Myths and Civilization of the
CELTS

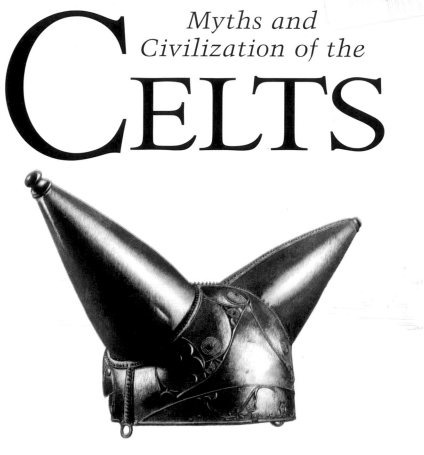

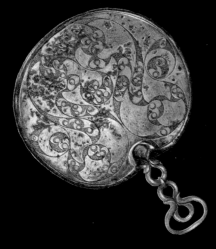

Published in the United States in 1999
by PETER BEDRICK BOOKS
A division of NTC/Contemporary Publishing Group, Inc.
4255 West Touhy Avenue, Lincolnwood (Chicago), Illinois
60646-1975 U.S.A.

The Myths & Civilization series
was created and produced by McRae Books,
via de' Rustici, 5 – Florence, Italy

Editors Anne McRae, Ronne Randall
Illustrations Francesca D'Ottavi (myths), Ivan Stalio, Alessandro Cantucci, Fabiano
Fabbrucci, Sauro Giampaia, Andrea Morandi (civilization)
Graphic Design Marco Nardi
Layout Vincenzo Cutugno, Ornella Fassio
Cutouts Adriano Nardi, Ornella Fassio
Color separations Litocolor., Florence (Italy)

Printed and bound in Italy by Grafiche Editoriali Padane, Cremona
International Standard Book Number: 0-87226-590-0

99   00   01   02   03   15   14   13   12   11   10   9   8   7   6   5   4   3   2   1

Myths and
Civilization of the
CELTS

Hazel Mary Martell

Illustrations by
Francesca D'Ottavi
Studio Stalio

PETER BEDRICK BOOKS
NEW YORK

CONTENTS

INTRODUCTION

The long history of the Celtic world has not come down to us in texts written by the Celts themselves. Instead, scholars have patched together the rather biased records left to us by their enemies, the Greeks and Romans, with the painstaking work of archeologists, to create a picture of one of the greatest of the early European peoples. Celtic tribes occupied much of continental Europe and the British Isles until the 1st century BC, when the Romans conquered almost all their lands. They left a rich store of burials, objects from everyday life, and works of art to intrigue future generations. We have also inherited many versions of their myths, initially preserved by Christian monks and then rewritten in medieval times. In this book we retell myths from different periods and explain how the Celts lived.

HOW THIS BOOK WORKS

This book is divided into sections, each of which begins with a myth and a striking illustration on a black background. This is followed by two pages focusing on an aspect of Celtic life related to the myth that precedes it.

The myth about how the Celts came to Ireland leads on to a non-fiction spread about who the Celts were and the origins of the Celtic world.

Unlike many other ancient peoples, the Celts did not leave a written record of their myths. What we know of Celtic mythology has been gathered from different sources, but scholars have no way of knowing how accurate this is. Classical writers, including Julius Caesar and Diodorus Siculus, recorded many Celtic rites and rituals, but not a lot about beliefs. The myths were first written down by monks in Ireland, but this happened very late when the Romans had already conquered most of the Celtic world and Christianity had been introduced. Even so, reading the myths alongside archeological facts about Celtic life helps bring this ancient people to life.

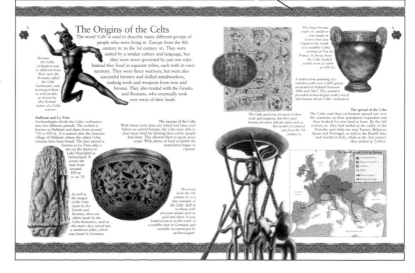

HOW THE CELTS CAME TO IRELAND

The Irish myths tell of five invasions of Ireland before the Celts. The first was led by Cessair, daughter of Noah's son, Bith. They arrived forty days before the Flood in which all but one of them drowned. The survivor was Fintan mac Bochra, who lived for 5,500 years, disguised as a salmon, an eagle, and a hawk, and saw all that followed.

The next invasion took place 300 years later and was led by Parthalon, who was descended from Noah's son, Japheth. In Ireland, however, Parthalon's people often had to fight their enemies, the Fomorians.

They were descended from Noah's son, Ham, and were fierce and monstrous beings, with only one arm and one leg each. But, before they could defeat the Fomorians, Parthalon, and all but one of his people died of plague.

Thirty years after Parthalon's invasion, Ireland was invaded again, this time by Nemedh and his followers. Their descendants attacked the Fomorians but were unsuccessful. Only thirty of them survived and they fled to Britain, the Northern Isles, and Greece. Their descendants led the next two invasions.

The first to arrive were the Fir Bholg from Greece. They ruled Ireland for 37 years and divided it into the provinces of Ulster, Leinster, Connacht, Munster, and Meath. The Tuatha De Danann, descendants of the people who fled to the Northern Isles, then invaded and defeated the Fir Bholg at the First Battle of Magh Tuiredh. In this battle, however, Nuadhu, the leader of the Tuatha De Danann, lost his right arm. This meant that he could no longer rule and his place was taken by Bres.

But Bres was a bad king and was forced to give up his throne. In revenge, he asked the Fomorians to gather an army. Meanwhile, the court physician made a silver arm for Nuadhu and he became king again. But his rule was brief – during a feast at Tara, he abdicated in favour of Lugh, a young warrior. Lugh led the Tuatha De Danann to victory against Bres at the Second Battle of Magh Tuiredh and drove the Fomorians into the sea.

After these five invasions, the Celts arrived. They landed in south-west Ireland and quickly defeated the Tuatha De Danann. Then they marched on Tara and defeated the Tuatha de Danann again, this time forcing them into exile.

The Origins of the Celts

The word "Celt" is used to describe many different groups of people who were living in Europe from the 8th century BC to the 1st century AD. They were united by a similar culture and language, but they were never governed by just one ruler. Instead they lived in separate tribes, each with its own territory. They were fierce warriors, but were also successful farmers and skilled metalworkers, making tools and weapons from iron and bronze. They also traded with the Greeks and Romans, who eventually took over most of their lands.

Because the Celtic civilization was so different from their own, the Romans called the Celts "barbarians" and portrayed them as wild people, as shown by this Roman statue of a Celtic warrior.

Hallstatt and La Tène

Archeologists divide the Celtic civilization into two different periods. The earliest is known as Hallstatt and dates from around 750 to 450 BC. It is named after the Austrian village of Hallstatt, where the oldest Celtic remains have been found. The later period is known as La Tène after a site on the shores of Lake Neuchâtel in Switzerland. It covers the time from around 450 BC to AD 50.

As well as the images of the Celts made by the Greeks and Romans, there are others made by the Celts themselves, such as this man's face carved into a sandstone pillar, which was found in Germany.

The success of the Celts

With better tools than any which had been used before in central Europe, the Celts were able to clear more land for farming than earlier people had done. This allowed them to grow more crops. With plenty of food available the population began to expand.

This bowl from the 5th century BC is a fine example of the Celts' skill in working with precious metals such as gold and silver. It was found in pieces in the tomb of a wealthy man in Germany and carefully reconstructed by archeologists.

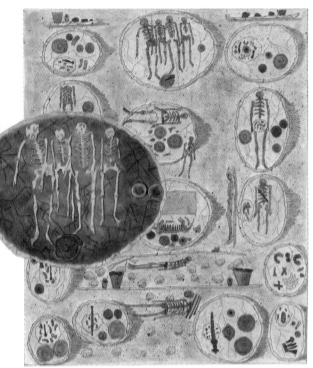

This huge bronze crater or cauldron was made in Greece but was found in the tomb of a wealthy Celtic woman at Vix in France. It shows how the Celts traded widely even as early as 600 BC.

A watercolor painting of a cemetery with over 1,000 graves excavated at Halstatt between 1846 and 1863. The cemetery provided archeologists with a lot of information about Celtic civilization.

The Celts used iron for most of their tools and weapons, but they used bronze for more delicate items such as this model of a funeral cart from the 7th century BC.

The spread of the Celts

The Celts and their civilization spread out over the centuries as their population expanded and they looked for new land to farm. By the 6th century BC they had settled in the valley of the Danube and what are now France, Belgium, Spain, and Portugal, as well as the British Isles and northern Italy, while in the 3rd century they settled in Turkey.

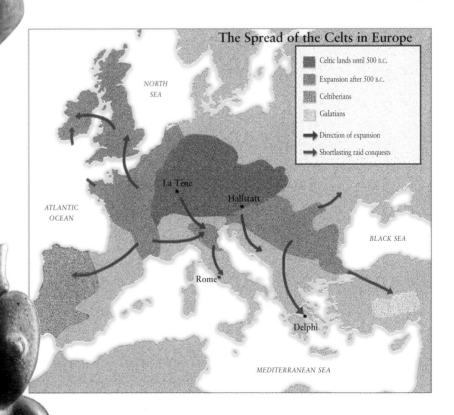

The Spread of the Celts in Europe

- Celtic lands until 500 B.C.
- Expansion after 500 B.C.
- Celtiberians
- Galatians
- → Direction of expansion
- → Shortlasting raid conquests

NORTH SEA

ATLANTIC OCEAN

La Tene

Hallstatt

BLACK SEA

Rome

Delphi

MEDITERRANEAN SEA

TALES FROM THE OTHERWORLD

The Celts believed there was another world beneath the one they lived in. Reached through underground caves and hollows in the hills, it was known as the Otherworld. It was inhabited by spirits and magical beings, as well as some of their gods and goddesses, and was also where people went to live after they had died in the human world. But this new life did not last for ever, as people could also die in the Otherworld. When this happened, they returned to the human world as babies and started life all over again.

However, it was not always necessary to die to pass from the human world to the Otherworld or back again. At certain times of the year it was possible to go from one to the other. The best time to do this was at the great festival of Samhain, which took place on 1 November and marked the start of winter and the Celtic new year. The night before Samhain was thought to belong neither to the old year nor to the new, and great armies of spirits from the Otherworld chose this time to visit the human world. They came in peace and often joined in the human celebrations.

Sometimes individuals came from the Otherworld to bestow a gift on a human, but this could not be used for personal gain. Instead, it had to be used to help other people. One such gift was given to Rhiwallon, the first doctor in the Welsh family known as the Physicians of Myddfai, when he was visited by the Lady of the Lake. She gave him a bag of herbs and recipes, and showed him a secret place where the herbs he would need for his medicines grew. She also gave him the gift of healing, which he was able to pass on to his sons.

On other occasions, humans were taken into the Otherworld to receive their gift. This happened to the piper of Dunmore in Galway, who, no matter how he tried, could only play one tune on his pipes. He played it one night as he was crossing over a bridge and the sound attracted an animal spirit, called the Puca na Samhna. This spirit grabbed hold of the piper and, carrying him on his back, took him to a great feast being held in the Otherworld. The piper was asked to provide the music for the evening's entertainment and easily played many different tunes. As a reward, he was given money and a new set of pipes, before being carried back to the bridge to continue his journey home. When he got there, he remembered the skills he had learnt in the Otherworld and from then onward he was the best piper in Ireland.

Religion and the Afterlife

Celtic religion was closely linked to nature and had many different gods and goddesses. The most important were worshiped by all the Celts, but others were special to just one tribe. Many were associated with streams, wells, trees, and rocks. Others were believed to bring success in warfare and hunting, and good harvests. The Celts offered sacrifices to their gods; these could be animals or humans, or gifts of flowers or jewelry. There were few formal temples and only the Celts in Britain and France had religious leaders, known as Druids. All Celts believed in life after death, and were usually buried with food and drink and some of their belongings.

Sacrificial shafts have been found in many of the Celtic lands. Up to 36 feet deep, they often contain human and animal bones and pottery.

The Druids were powerful men who performed religious ceremonies and made sacrifices on behalf of their tribes. It took them up to twenty years to gain the knowledge they needed for this.

The Druids believed that mistletoe had special magic powers.

Epona, the horse goddess
One of the most important and best-known of the Celtic goddesses was Epona. She was worshiped from early times and, as well as being the goddess of horses, she was the goddess of fertility and good harvests. Sacrifices in her honor were thought to help bring good crops.

This figure of Epona was found in France. It shows her as a woman leading a horse, but in other figures the horse itself represents the goddess.

A gold model of a Celtic boat from Ireland, probably made as an offering to the sea god, Manannan mac Lir.

This god from the 1st century BC shows his strength by holding up two men. Each man holds a boar, while other animals stand on the god's shoulders.

CELTIC BURIALS

The Celts believed that after people died they went to another world which was very much like this one. They were therefore buried with objects that they might need there, as well as items that would be useful on the journey. The wealthy man in this tomb at Hochdorf in Germany even had a wagon buried with him, together with a huge cauldron, and drinking horns and dishes for nine people. His body was laid out on a large bronze couch. A comb and a razor were left by his head, while on his feet he wore sandals decorated with gold.

Sacred sites and sacrifices

The Celts had many sacred sites associated with their gods. These were often lakes or streams, but in Britain and France there were also sacred groves of oak trees. Only the Druids were allowed to go there to cut the mistletoe, which grew on the oak trees and was thought to have magic qualities. Both humans and animals were sometimes sacrificed in the sacred groves, but it was more common for valued possessions to be offered to the gods in exchange for favors.

Same gods – different names

Celts in different parts of Europe often had different names for the same god. For example, the Gauls called their sun god Belenos, while in Germany he was Beel, in Ireland he was Bile, and in Wales he was Beli Mawr. Similarly the sea god was called Manannan mac Lir in Ireland, Manawydden in Wales, and Shony in Scotland.

The Celts made many different images of a god with horns. This one is carved in sandstone and dates from around 500 BC. Found in Germany, it probably represents Cernunnos, who was the ruler of the animals and possibly also of the Otherworld.

THE LEGEND OF MAON

Maon was the great-grandson of the legendary Ugainy the Great, who ruled over the whole of Ireland and a large part of Western Europe. With his Gaulish wife, Kesair, Ugainy had two sons, Laery and Covac. When Laery inherited the kingdom after Ugainy's death, Covac was so filled with jealousy that he became ill. He knew that the only way he could take the kingdom from Laery was by killing him, but whenever Covac met Laery, Laery always had an armed escort with him.

Finally a Druid advised Covac to pretend that he had died and send a message to Laery, inviting him to the burial. Covac did this, and when Laery and his son Ailill came to see the body, Covac quickly jumped up and stabbed them both to death.

Covac's illness then left him, but he could not forget the jealousy he had felt toward his brother. So, as a final revenge, he took Ailill's young son, Maon, and made him eat a part of Laery's heart and a part of Ailill's heart, before forcing him to swallow a mouse and her babies. This upset Maon so much that he could no longer speak and, realizing that the child was no longer a threat to him, Covac sent him away to live with the ruler of Feramorc and his daughter Moriath.

From Feramorc Maon went to Gaul to live with his great-grandmother's people and there he grew into a fine young man.

Meanwhile Moriath, who had fallen in love with him, did not forget the handsome young Maon. She was determined that he would come back to Ireland and regain his kingdom.

She wrote a love song for him and sent her father's harpist to sing it to him. Maon was so moved that his speech returned and, with the help of his grandmother's people, he raised an army and sailed to Ireland to find Covac. After a long search he found his old enemy and forced him to fight for the kingdom.

The battle took place at Dinrigh and Maon was victorious, killing Covac along with many of his nobles and warriors. Having reclaimed his kingdom, Maon married Moriath, the woman whose love had helped to make his victory possible.

Society and Everyday Life

The Celts were divided into many different tribes, each of which had its own leader. This was usually a man, but could also be a woman. Within each tribe, there were four classes of people. They were the nobles, the warriors, the farmers, and the learned people. This last group included Druids, metalworkers, poets, and storytellers. Many people belonged to more than one social class, however, as farmers had to be warriors at times, while learned men had to do some farming as well. Each tribe was spread over a large area and the people within it lived in small communities, rather than large settlements.

Writing
This carving is one of the few written records from Celtic times, as the Druids discouraged people from learning to read or write in case they became too powerful. Most information was passed on by word of mouth.

Farm animals
As well as growing cereal crops and vegetables in the fields around their homes, Celtic farmers kept pigs and cattle for their meat and their skins, which could be turned into leather. Cattle also provided milk, while oxen could be used to pull a plow or a cart. Hens, ducks, and geese were kept for their eggs and feathers, while swarms of bees were kept to provide honey.

Everyday meals
Cereals were an important part of the Celtic diet and grinding grain into flour to make bread was an everyday task. Grain was also used in stews and porridge, as well as being fermented to make beer. Onions, peas, beans, and lentils were added to the stews which were cooked in large iron cauldrons. The food was served on dishes made from wood or earthenware. It was eaten with the fingers or a chunk of bread, as there were no forks and only a few spoons. Drink was served from large jugs, but only a wealthy person would have one as richly decorated as the one shown here.

A CARING SOCIETY
Although the Celts were famous for their warlike nature and are known to have traded in slaves, there was also a caring side to their society. Any members of the tribe who had no family and were too old, ill, or weak to support themselves were looked after by others, who provided shelter, warmth, clothing, and food. The Celts also tried to heal the sick and the injured by using herbs to make medicines and ointments, as well as by making sacrifices. Among the learned men in society there were doctors and surgeons who knew how to set broken bones and perform simple operations, using alcohol as a painkiller and antiseptic.

Iron sieve

Iron cup

Many Celtic farming tools were similar to those used in the early 20th century (and still used in many parts of the world). This sickle with its iron blade and wooden handle was used to cut down cereal crops when they were ripe.

Sickle

Knife

Cooking utensils
Many Celtic women spent a large part of each day preparing food and cooking it over an open fire. Most of their utensils were made from iron, but wood and earthenware were also used for dishes and containers.

Long-bladed knives like this one had many uses around the farm. For example, it could be used to cut up fodder and bedding for animals that were kept inside over the winter or to chop up reeds or straw to thatch the roofs of buildings.

Houses
Celtic houses were often round, though some were square or oblong. The walls were made from stone, panels of wattle and daub, or upright wooden planks. Reeds, straw, or heather were used for the roof, which sloped steeply so that rain or snow would run off quickly.

Sheep shears

The importance of sheep
Sheep were kept for their wool and milk, but were very rarely eaten. Like pigs and cattle, they were smaller, thinner, and hairier than the same animals today.

Three-pronged fish spear

Hunting and fishing
Many Celts varied their diet by hunting wild boar and deer in the woodlands and forests which surrounded their farms. Those who lived near the sea or by lakes and rivers went fishing, using nets or spears.

Around the hearth
Most Celtic houses had just one big room in which the whole family ate and slept and did their daily chores. In the center was the hearth with an open fire, which provided heat and light, and was also used for cooking. There were no windows and usually only one door, protected by a porch on the outside. This helped to keep out the drafts that could make sparks fly from the hearth and set the house on fire. The floor was made of hardened mud, but there is little evidence of any furniture. People probably wrapped themselves in animal skins to sleep and kept items they were not using on shelves or hooks on the walls.

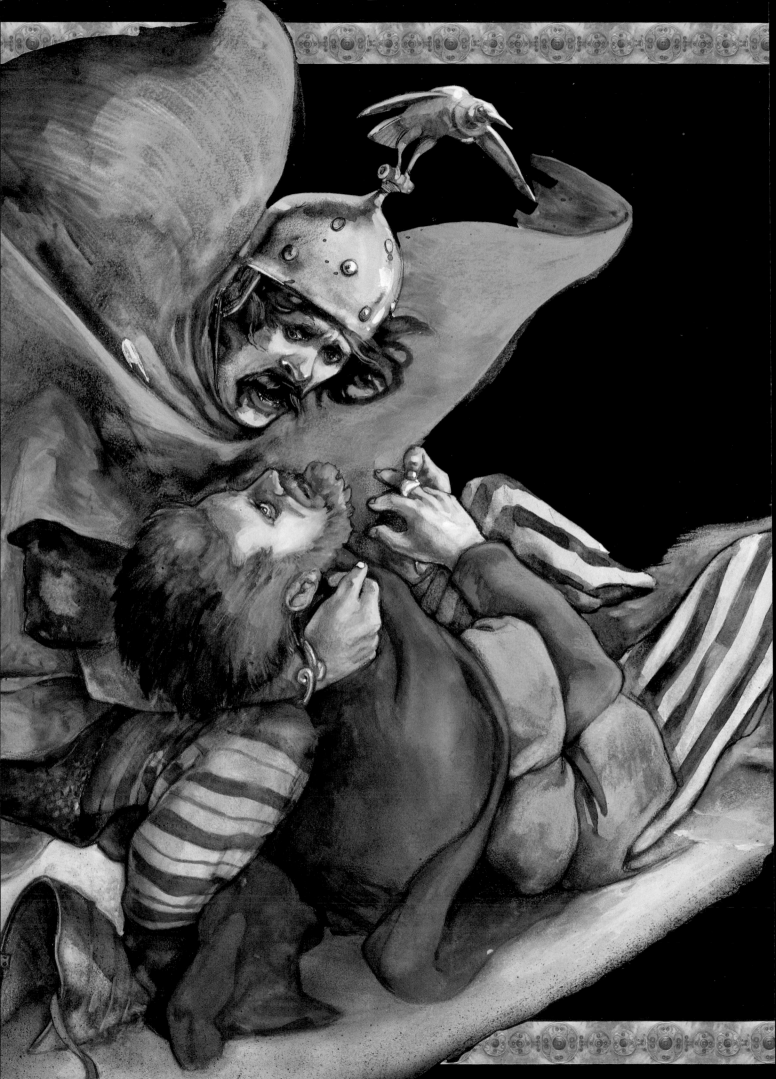

THE TRAGEDY OF CUCHULAIN

When Cuchulain, the great hero of Ulster, was a young man, he fell in love with a beautiful woman called Emer. She refused to marry him until he proved himself in battle.

Determined to do this, Cuchulain traveled to the Land of Shadows where the fierce and mighty she-warrior, Skatha, lived. He asked her to teach him her skills and she agreed. While he was there, Skatha declared war on Aoife, the most powerful she-warrior in the world. When their armies met, Cuchulain and two of Skatha's sons killed six of Aoife's best warriors. But Aoife knew that she was stronger than Skatha and so she challenged her to fight in single combat. Then Cuchulain offered to fight in Skatha's place and, defeating Aoife by trickery, he threw her over his shoulder and carried her back to Skatha's camp. The two women soon made peace, and Cuchulain and Aoife became friends and then lovers. But Cuchulain could only stay in the Land of Shadows for a year and a day and, by the time he had to leave, Aoife was expecting his child. Cuchulain gave her a gold ring and told her that, if the child were a boy, she was to call him Connla and give him the ring when he was big enough and then send him in search of his father.

Aoife agreed to this, but after Connla was born she heard that Cuchulain had married Emer. Overcome by jealousy, she decided to have her revenge. When the time came for Connla to go in search of his father, she made him promise not to tell anyone his name, not to turn his back, and never to refuse a challenge.

All went well until he reached Ulster where King Conor and his noblemen were gathered on the beach. Looking out to sea, they saw a boat with golden oars approaching. Not knowing the young man in it, Conor told him to turn back, but he refused to do so. Conor then sent his fiercest warriors to challenge him, but he defeated them one by oneo.

Finally Conor sent Cuchulain to fight the stranger. The fight was long and at one point Cuchulain almost drowed. Then he remembered the Gae Bholg, a special weapon that Skatha had given him. He quickly threw it and the stranger fell, fatally wounded. As Cuchulain pulled him from the water, he saw the ring on the young man's finger and realized that he had just killed Connla, his only son.

Clothing and Jewels

Greek and Roman writers were very struck by the appearance of the Celts, whom they described as tall, with shaggy blonde or red hair, large moustaches and pale skins. They were also impressed by the bright, colorful clothing and ornate jewelry they wore.

The gold bracelet and earrings shown here were made in the 4th century BC. They were found in a large tomb in France and would have belonged to a wealthy Celtic woman.

Clothing

Celtic men wore long or short-sleeved tunics or shirts over trousers. Women wore long robes made from two rectangles of fabric fastened up the sides and held at the shoulders by a pair of *fibulae* (buckles). Simple wrap-around skirts have also been found. Most clothing was spun from linen or wool, although some very rich people had garments made from imported silk. Remnants of cloth show that bold checked patterns, similar to tartans, were often worn.

Chain-mail tunic and ornate sword, worn by aristocratic warriors. The man also has blue tattoos on his arms, typical of English Celtic warriors.

Tartan cloaks spun from wool for warmth.

All three members of this family are wearing jewelry.

This ornate silver fibula (buckle) would have been one of a pair used by a Celtic woman to fasten her dress at the shoulder.

This illustration shows what a wealthy family of English Celts may have looked like. Celtic women wore their hair long. Both men and women wore jewelry. The fact that the men wore trousers was considered uncouth by the Greeks and Romans, although they were probably very practical in the cool climate of northern Europe.

Jewelry

Celtic men and women wore jewelry, including bracelets, armlets, anklets, and necklaces. Rings and earrings were less common among the Celts before the Roman conquest. Jewelry was made from bronze, often covered with enamel, as well as gold, glass, coral, and amber, which were often fashioned into beads.

This stone statue of a man's head and neck (probably of a god), shows the typical Celtic fashion – a moustache and a heavy gold torque around the neck.

Reconstruction of a Celtic loom.

Making cloth

The Celts kept sheep for wool and harvested flax, which they made into linen. The wool was spun on a wooden spindle then woven into cloth on an upright loom. We don't really know who spun the wool and wove it into clothing; it may have been a woman's occupation.

This glass and amber necklace comes from a tomb in France. It dates from the 5th century BC.

THE ORIGINS OF TARTAN

The Greek historian Diodorus Siculus wrote of Celtic dress: "The clothing they wear is striking – shirts which have been dyed and embroidered in various colors, and breeches, which they call *bracae*; and they wear striped cloaks, fastened by a brooch on the shoulder, heavy for winter wear and light in the summer, in which are placed checks, close together and of many different colors." In the last sentence, he is clearly describing an early form of tartan.

Gold torques, like this one, were worn around the neck by men and women of high rank.

THE DAGDA'S PORRIDGE BOWL

The Dagda was one of the great chieftains of the legendary Tuatha De Danann. He was also the most important god of the Celts in Ireland. His name means the "good god," but he was also known as the "father of all" and "lord of perfect knowledge." His possessions included a cauldron that never ran out of food, and a magic pig that could be killed and eaten, then come alive again ready to be killed and eaten again the next day. He also had a magic club – with one end he could kill nine men with a single blow, and with a touch of the other end he could restore them to life.

As well as being the god of wisdom, the Dagda was also the god of the earth and enjoyed earthly pleasures. He was fond of music and played his harp to bring about the change in the seasons. He also enjoyed feasting and being in the company of beautiful women. The Dagda's enemies, the Fomorians, used this knowledge to try to prevent him from fighting against them in the Second Battle of Magh Tuiredh.

During a truce in the battle, the Fomorians found the Dagda resting and began mocking him over his great appetite. They challenged him to eat a meal of porridge, his favorite food, which they would cook for him. The Dagda accepted the challenge, and the preparations started.

As the Fomorians did not have a big enough cooking pot, they dug a hole in the ground and poured into it 80 cauldrons full of fresh milk, 80 cauldrons of oats, and 80 cauldrons of fat. To this they added whole sheep, pigs, and goats. The porridge was then boiled, and when it was ready, the Fomorians gave the Dagda an enormous spoon and told him to eat every scrap or be killed.

To their amazement, the Dagda did just this and, to make sure nothing was left behind, he used his finger to scrape the last drops out of the hole. After such a big meal, the Fomorians expected the Dagda to fall asleep and miss the rest of the battle, but instead he stayed wide awake.

Then the Fomorians remembered his love of beautiful women. They brought him a lovely young woman and left her in his company. They thought this would exhaust him, but once more they were wrong. The Dagda was soon revitalized and ready to return to battle. The young woman was so pleased with him that she took his side and helped him to defeat the Fomorians.

Feasting and Entertainment

Celtic festivals were held to mark the changing of the seasons and were tied in with the fertility of the earth and of livestock. The four main festivals were: Imbolg, in February to mark the beginning of spring; Beltane, in May to mark the onset of summer; Lughnasad, the harvest feast in July and August; and Samhain, which means "summer," although the festival was held at the end of summer on November 1. On these occasions, but also on many others, the Celts held banquets where lashings of food and drink were served, and bards and musicians entertained the guests.

Pieces of a Gaulish calendar from about 10 BC found in France. It records the month of Samhain (summer), from mid-October to mid-November, which marked the summer's end and the Celtic New Year.

The cauldron was synonymous with feasting for the Celts and became a symbol of abundance for them.

Banqueting etiquette

At feasts the guests were seated according to their rank, with the most important man in the center with the host next to him. On either side sat the next most important guests, and so on round the circle. The banquet was important for the host because it gave him a chance to show how rich he was by the abundance of food and wine served.

BANQUETS

Celtic feasts could be wild affairs. Large quantities of alcohol – wine, beer, and mead – were served in cups which were continually passed around. When the banqueters were very drunk, fights sometimes broke out during which, if we are to believe Greek observers, people were occasionally killed. The Greeks also commented unfavorably on the Celts' table manners. Diodorus Siculus tells us "...when they are eating, their moustaches become entangled in their food, and when they are drinking, the beverage passes, as it were, through a kind of strainer."

During the banquet musicians and bards sang, played instruments, and recited stories and poems. The lyre and pipes were common musical instruments. The scene (left) shows two musicians seated on an ornate couch.

Sports

The Celts played team games, including hurley, which is still played in Ireland and the Scottish Highlands today, as well as an early form of hockey. During the festival of Lughnasad in July and August, the Celtic tribes gathered and sporting competitions were held. The All Ireland Games were held in Tara each year at this time.

Hunting

Hunting was a favorite sport among well-off Celts. They kept special hunting dogs for the purpose. They hunted wild boar, deer, wolves, foxes, badgers, hares, and rabbits. The meat was eaten and the pelts were used to make clothing. This huntsman is mounted on a horse and he and his dog are pursuing a wild boar. The bell on the horse's neck may have served to frighten prey out of the undergrowth.

In times of peace Celtic warriors engaged in horse and chariot racing, which were good training for wars.

The Celts loved to drink wine. They imported it from Italy, often paying the merchants very high prices. One record shows that a slave was exchanged for a jar of wine. These jugs for storing wine are from Germany.

The Celts liked to play table games, such as brandub, for which they used little glass marbles like the ones shown left. The Celts also played a game very similar to chess, called fidchell.

THE TALE OF PEREDUR

Peredur, a seventh son, was marked out by destiny for strange and high fortunes. His father and six brothers had all been slain in war, so his mother brought him up in a forest where he could learn nothing of warfare. But one evening Peredur saw three knights from Arthur's court in the forest. Entranced by the sight, he asked his mother who the men were. "They are angels, my son," she said. "Then I will go and become an angel with them," he replied. Peredur's mother could not discourage him, so in the end she gave him her blessing and told him to seek the Court of Arthur, where lived the best and boldest of knights.

Peredur set out on a bony piebald work horse, his only weapons a handful of sharp-pointed stakes. When he arrived at Arthur's castle he was rudely repulsed by the steward, Kai, for his rustic appearance. To win entrance, Peredur had to fight a ruffian knight who had offended the court. Peredur beat the knight and took his armor, weapons, and horse.

Setting out on his own, he came to a castle by a lake. Peredur entered the castle where he was received by a very old man. After eating, the man said "I am your uncle, your mother's brother." When he left, the old man warned him never to ask the meaning of whatever might puzzle him if no one saw fit to explain it to him.

Peredur rode until he came to the Castle of Wonders. He entered the great hall and was received by the lord. After dining, the lord asked Peredur if he knew how to use a sword. "If I were to receive instruction," said Peredur, "I think I could." The lord gave Perdur a sword and told him to strike an iron staple in the floor. Peredur did so and cut the staple in two. But the sword also flew into two parts. "Put the two parts together," said the lord. Peredur did so and they were one again. A second time this was done with the same result. The third time neither the sword nor the staple would reunite. "Your have reached two-thirds of your strength," said the lord. Then he too declared that he was Peredur's uncle. As they spoke, two youths entered the hall carrying a lance dripping with blood. Next came two maidens carrying a glowing silver dish on which lay a man's severed head. The whole party began to wail and lament. Peredur did not ask for an explanation, but went to bed.

Later he learnt that the head in the silver dish belonged to a cousin and the lance was the weapon used to slay him. Peredur had been shown these things so that he would avenge them. The evil had been done to Peredur's family by the nine sourceresses of Gloucester. With Arthur's help, Peredur slew all nine and vengeance was accomplished.

The Celts at War

Celtic armies struck fear into the hearts of their opponents when they first appeared in the ancient world. Carrying arms and demonstrating courage and bravery were important symbols of manhood among the Celts, and war was the perfect opportunity to show these qualities. In the early times, the Celts fought among themselves, resolving family feuds and forging new tribal relationships, as well as against the peoples they encountered as they spread across Europe. In Roman times, they amassed huge armies in an attempt to defeat the expanding Roman Empire. However, they were no match for the well-armed and disciplined troops from Rome and were soon subdued.

Until about 200 BC many Celtic warriors fought naked. Their bodies decorated with tattoos and carrying only their weapons, they fell upon their enemies.

Celtic armor

The Celts used no armor at all until about 300 BC when they invented chain-mail (which the Romans soon copied). However, a suit of chain-mail was very expensive and only aristocratic warriors could afford one. Most warriors fought in breeches and shirt, like the statue of the warrior god shown here. Note the torque around his neck.

Battle tactics

When the Celts were face to face with their enemies, they formed a line of battle, grouped by clan. Sometimes, prominent warriors challenged the foes' leaders to hand-to-hand combat before the main battle began. Meanwhile the rest of the warriors worked themselves into a frenzy with battle songs, chants and horn playing, and often drinking large amounts of alcohol. They made a tremendous din, before hurling themselves at their enemy (who sometimes fled in terror before the fighting even began).

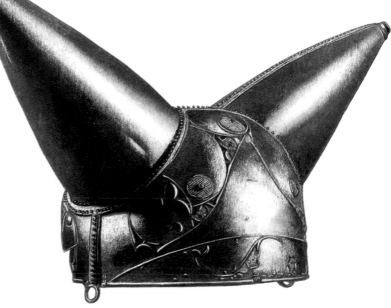

"On their heads they wear bronze helmets which possess large projecting fingers lending the appearance of enormous stature to their wearer." Diodorus Siculus.

This coin shows a Celtic warrior terrorizing the enemy in his war chariot.

Most shields were made of flat wooden boards lined with leather. Since the Celts loved bright colors and elaborate decorations, they were probably painted with colorful symbols and patterns. The Battersea Shield (right) is a fine example of Celtic craftsmanship. Cast in bronze (with glass inlays) in the 1st century AD, it was found in the River Thames in 1857.

Weapons

Celtic warriors all carried a long spear and a shield. Wealthier Celts would also have carried a sword and worn a protective metal helmet and a shirt of chain-mail. The Celts also used bows and arrows and slings in battle.

Cavalry

As the use of chariots declined in about 200 BC, more and more Celtic warriors fought from horseback. They had a special four-pommelled saddle which allowed them to fight effectively while mounted even though they did not use stirrups. The beautiful riding horses of Gaul and Spain made excellent warhorses.

THE BATTLE OF TELAMON

The Celts and Romans fought one their greatest battles in central Italy in 225 BC. The Celtic army of 50,000 infantry and 20,000 chariots was trapped between two Roman armies at Telamon. The Roman historian Polybius described the scene: "... encouraged by having caught the enemy between their two armies ... [the Romans were also] terrified by the fine order of the Celtic host and the dreadful din, for there were innumerable trumpeters and horn-blowers, and ... the whole army shouting their war cries at the same time ... The Romans attacked [and] though being almost cut to pieces, the Celts held their ground, equal to their foes in courage, and inferior only in their arms ... About 40,000 Celts were slain and at least 10,000 taken prisoner."

Chariots

Early Celtic armies were composed of large numbers of chariots. These were single-axled vehicles, drawn by two ponies and carrying a driver and a warrior. They raced about the field even before the battle began, hurling javelins and creating vast amounts of noise and uproar to dishearten their opponents.

Reconstruction of a Celtic chariot.

How Cuchulain Got His Name

The smith was a very important person in Celtic society. Everyone depended on his skills for the tools and weapons they needed to survive. Most smiths worked in small communities, making simple objects for everyday use. However, the best of them worked at court, making weapons and beautiful objects in silver and gold for the king and his closest companions.

One of the most famous smiths was Culann, who worked at the court of King Conchobar. Culann was so rich that he could afford to give a feast splendid enough to invite the king himself. At that time the king was looking after his foster son, Sedanta, who was seven years old, and so he invited the boy to go with him to the feast. Sedanta was busy playing with his friends, however, and so he told the king he would follow him to Culann's house when he had finished his game.

By the time the king and his courtiers reached Culann's house, dusk was falling, and as Culann invited them in and the feast began, Sedanta was quite forgotten. The gates to the house were securely barred and Culann let his favorite hound loose in the grounds to protect his property and his guests from would-be robbers and other wrongdoers.

All went well until halfway through the evening. Suddenly the mighty barking of the hound was heard above the sound of merrymaking, warning Culann that a stranger was approaching his house. As his guests fell quiet and listened, the barking changed to howling and then to silence.

Puzzled by this, Culann and his guests ran out to see what had happened. They found Sedanta at the gate with the hound lying dead at his feet; he had killed it with his bare hands after it had attacked him. Culann's guests praised Sedanta for his bravery, but Culann himself was sad over the death of his favorite hound, which had only been trying to protect him.

Seeing the smith's sorrow, Sedanta asked to be given a puppy from the same strain as the hound and promised he would train it himself until it was as good as the dog he had killed. When Culann agreed to this, Sedanta made him another promise. Asking for a shield and a spear, he said he would guard Culann as well as any dog until the puppy was completely trained. Culann accepted the offer and from that day onward Sedanta became known as Cuchulain, which means "the hound of Culann."

Art and Crafts

The earliest Celtic artisans at Halstatt decorated the metal and ceramic objects they made with simple geometric designs or with parallel lines or circles. From about 500 BC, when trade with Mediterranean peoples increased and the Celts came into contact with Classical designs, a new artistic style gradually developed. It is known as La Tène style, after an important archeological site in Switzerland. La Tène art is full of lovely whorls and elegant curved lines. Celtic artists did not compose scenes showing lifelike portraits of people, as their Greek and Roman counterparts did. Instead, people are usually only represented by stylized faces, and animals are also shown in very stylized ways. Some people have compared Celtic art with that of the famous 20th-century artist, Pablo Picasso.

This statue shows a blacksmith-god at work in his forge. Smiths were quite highly regarded in Celtic society because of the range of essential items they made, including, for example, cooking vessels, farm tools, wheels, weapons, and jewelry.

Mines

The iron and ores needed to make different metals first had to be mined and then shipped to the places where they were used. The best iron was said to come from Noricum in Austria, while tin (used to make bronze) had to be brought from Cornwall, in England. The best gold was mined in the Pyrenees, in Spain.

Horses and human faces were among the most common decorations on Celtic coins. This gold stater was made by a Celtic tribe that lived in northern Gaul and moved to southern Britain after the Roman invasion of Gaul.

Early Celtic craftspeople at Hallstatt made these sturdy leather rucksacks. They were used by salt miners to carry the salt. Over 2,000 years old, they were preserved by the salt.

The Celtic wheel

The Celts learnt to make very sturdy, hard-wearing wheels, which they used on carts and chariots. They were the result of cooperation between carpenters and blacksmiths. Celtic carpenters learned to make the "felloe," or outer rim of the wheel, from of a single piece of wood. Blacksmiths covered this with a heated iron tyre that shrank as it cooled, compressing the wooden rim and spokes and making the wheel exceptionally strong.

This beautiful bronze mirror is decorated on the back with elaborate symmetrical designs. It was found in Desborough, England and was made by Celtic craftspeople in about 100 BC.

In just a few simple lines, the artist has captured the spirit of the horse. This was probably used as a chariot-fitting, and was made in the 1st century AD.

Blacksmiths decorated some of their wares by inserting glass or coral inlays. They also learnt to fuse glass with the surface of copper and developed enamel work. Red was a favorite color for these decorations, but as the craft developed many different colors were used.

These horse trappings are made of cast bronze, with enamel insets.

Pottery

From the beginning of the La Tène period in the 5th century BC, craftspeople in mainland Europe used pottery wheels to make pots. They also had sophisticated kilns and could vary the color of the vessels they made from red to grey or black. In Britain, potters continued to make their pots by hand.

THE SWORD IN THE STONE

The legends of King Arthur tell us that after the death of Uther Pendragon there was no king in England. Though Uther Pendragon had had a son, he was only a baby when his father died and Merlin the Magician had spirited him away to a foster home until the time was right for him to reveal himself as the true king. The country fell into chaos as the nobles fought each other for the title and there was no one to enforce the laws of the land. Things went from bad to worse, then Merlin came up with an idea.

He produced a huge stone, in which was a sword. Gold letters around the stone said that whoever could pull out the sword was the true king by right of birth. Many tried, but no one could move the sword. Finally it was decided that every noble in the land should be given a chance to remove the sword and a date was set for them all to compete.

Among the nobles who went on that day was Ector, with his son Kay and foster son Arthur. When they arrived, however, Kay realized that he had left his own sword at home and asked Arthur to go and fetch it for him. Arthur went, but when he got to the house, the door was locked. Not wanting to let his foster brother down, Arthur remembered the sword in the stone and decided to take that for Kay instead.

Arthur pulled it out easily, but Kay recognized the sword and took it to show his father. Ector called for Arthur and asked him if any one had seen him remove it. Arthur replied that he had been alone at the time and so Ector told him to go back to the stone and replace the sword. When Arthur had done this, Ector then tried to pull the sword out himself, but he could not move it. Kay also tried, but without success. Arthur then tried again and once more pulled it out with no effort.

Ector realized that his foster son must really be the son of Uther Pendragon, though he knew it would be difficult to persuade the other noblemen to accept this and allow Arthur to rule over them. Three more competitions were organized and at each one Arthur was the only person who could pull the sword from the stone. The noblemen would still not accept him, however, and so a fourth competition was held and this time the common people were also invited. When they saw Arthur pull the sword from the stone, they at once accepted him as king and he was crowned the very same day.

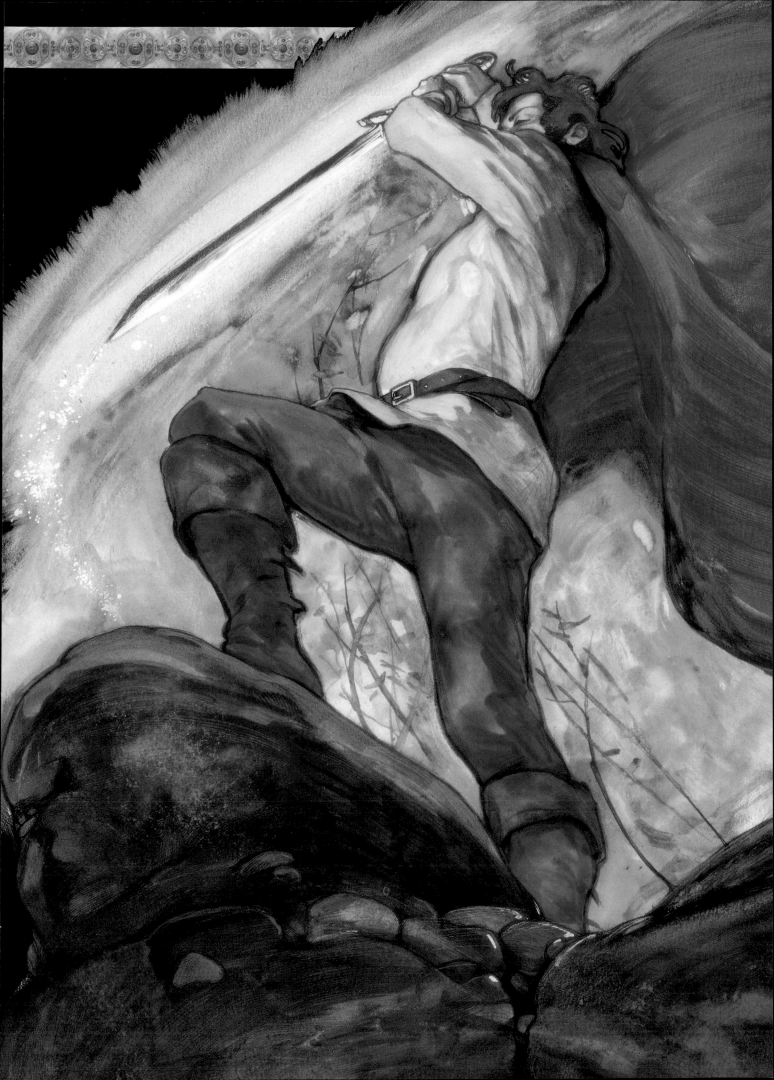

Wine was a staple Celtic import. Roman traders hauled it up the rivers of central Europe in small barges like the one in this carving.

Trade and Transport

The Celts had a well-developed network of trade routes throughout Europe and the Mediterranean. They exported slaves, furs, gold, iron, salt, and foodstuffs (salt-cured Celtic meats were considered a great delicacy in Rome) south to the Mediterranean. In return they imported wine, Greek and Etruscan vases, ornate jewelry and other luxury goods produced in southern Europe. Most of the goods traveled by river, mainly up the Rhône and the Saône. The city of Massilia (present day Marseilles), at the mouth of the Rhône, became an important meeting point and market town. Although we know from Roman accounts that the Celts also had ocean-going sea vessels, archeologists have only found and studied riverboats. The Celts also traveled overland by foot, on horseback, and in two- or four-wheeled carts.

This large oak statue of a protective god overlooked the Celtic port of Geneva. The town that grew up around the port was the basis of the modern city.

This four-wheeled cart was found in a princely tomb. The wooden frame is entirely covered with iron. It was complete with yoke and reins for two horses when found.

THE BRITISH TIN TRADE

Celtic Britain was largely self-sufficient and had only limited contact with continental Europe. The exception to this was Cornwall, with its rich tin mines. Tin was an essential component in making bronze, and traders from all over Europe flocked to the area from earliest times. In the words of Diodorus Siculus: "The inhabitants of Britain who live on the promontory of Belerion [Cornwall] are especially hospitable to strangers and have adopted a very civilized manner because of their continual meetings with merchants and other peoples ... they work tin into pieces the size of knucklebones and convey it to an island which lies off Britain and is called Ictis ... On the island the merchants purchase the tin from the natives and carry it from there across the Strait to Gaul; and finally, making their way on foot through Gaul for some 30 days, they bring their wares on horseback to the mouth of the River Rhône."

This pick was used to mine salt. The white stone was used to sharpen the blade.

Ideas as well as goods traveled along the trade routes. For example, the Celts learnt to make glass from Mediterranean peoples. They were soon able to create their own distinctive glassware objects, like this tiny blue, white, and yellow statue of a dog.

Salt

Salt was an important commodity for the Celts. Before refrigerators were invented salting was the only way to preserve meat, fish, and many other products for any length of time. There were numerous salt mines in Gaul and throughout the Celtic world. Many of the salt-preserved Celtic products were exported.

Gold coin from Gaul, showing an image of Philip of Macedonia.

The design on the neck of this Hallstatt jug show signs of the influence of Mediterranean peoples on Celtic artisans.

Buying and selling

The Celts only began to make coins after they came into contact with the Greeks, some time after about 700 BC. Before that time, and probably for a long time after, the traded goods were exchanged for items of equal value. The Celts are thought to have used their beautiful metalwork objects to pay for valuable commodities from their trading partners.

THE CHILDREN OF LIR

Lir was a chieftain of the Tuatha De Danaan who lived at Finaghy in the north of Ireland. When his wife died, his ruler, Bov Dearg, invited Lir to his court and suggested he marry one of his three foster-daughters. Lir agreed and chose Eve, the eldest of the three. They went back to Finaghy where, after a year of marriage, Eve gave birth to twins, Fionnuala and Aedh, a girl and a boy. A year later, Eve gave birth to twin sons, Fiachra and Conn, but she died in childbirth.

Lir was heartbroken and only the love of his four children kept him alive. Then Bov Dearg invited Lir again and suggested that he marry Eve's sister, Aoife. Lir agreed and at first things went well. Aoife loved the children and they loved her. But gradually she came to think that Lir loved his children more than he loved her. One day Aoife took the children to visit Bov Dearg. Three times on the journey Aoife stopped her chariot and told her servants to kill the children, but they refused. On the shores of Lough Derravaragh she stopped again and told the children to go and bathe in the lake. As they did so she cast a spell, turning them into swans but leaving them their human voices.

When Fionnuala asked how long the spell would last, Aoife realized what a terrible thing she had done. The children would spend 300 years on Lough Derravaragh, 300 years on the wild Sea of Moyle and then 300 years on lonely Inish Gluaire, before regaining their human bodies - when the sound of a bell would start to change Ireland.

The children bore their punishment bravely. For the first 300 years they had many visitors who brought them news of their friends and family and listened to their sweet singing. On the Sea of Moyle the visitors were fewer and on Inish Gluaire they saw no one at all.

Finally the day came for the spell to end and, still in the shape of swans, they flew back to their home. As they landed, a Christian monk rang a bell, inviting people to join the new religion and pray. As Aoife promised, this broke the spell, but when Lir's children changed back to their human forms, they were no longer young. Instead they were more than 900 years old and everything they had known and loved when they were human before had gone. All that remained was their love for each other, and as the saint blessed them, they linked arms and died.

The Waning of Celtic Civilization

As Roman civilization expanded in the last centuries BC, first in Italy and then into Gaul (France), the Celts were either conquered and forced to live under Roman domination, or they fled north and west. The Celts did not give in without a fight and there were many brutal wars. Julius Caesar led the first Roman expedition into Britain in 55 BC, although the Romans did not occupy Britain until almost a century later. By the 2nd century AD most of the Celtic lands had been absorbed by the Roman Empire. Fortunately for the Celts, the Empire lacked the strength to expand further and a few Celtic strongholds survived in Ireland, Wales, and the Scottish Highlands.

Statue showing a Roman horseman riding roughshod over the "barbarian" Celts.

AN ENGLISH QUEEN REVOLTS

The Iceni in East Anglia had become a client state of the Romans under their king, Prasutagus. When he died in AD 60, power passed to his wife, Boudicca, and their daughters. However, the Romans did not recognize them as leaders and tried to incorporate the area into the Roman Empire as a province. Boudicca led a huge army of Celts against the Romans, hoping to drive them back across the Channel into Gaul. A pitched battle was fought somewhere in the Midlands, but the Celts lost. In keeping with Celtic tradition, brave Boudicca is said to have died by her own hand shortly after losing the battle.

Celtic leader Vercingetorix led a revolt against the Roman invaders in Gaul (modern France) in 52 BC. After a heroic struggle, he was forced to surrender. Vercingetorix was executed in Rome after being paraded through the city's streets.

This famous Roman statue (a copy of a 2nd-century BC bronze by Attalus of Pergamon) is called the Dying Gaul. *It actually shows a Galatian (the Celts who inhabited present-day Turkey) warrior, nursing a fatal wound. We can see that he is a Celt because of his spiky hair, the gold torque at his neck, and the fact that he is naked. Celtic warriors of the early period often fought naked and they also caked their hair in lime, making it stick out, a bit like 20th-century punks.*

The Irish monks also produced some very beautiful illustrated manuscripts. These are a wonderful mixture of Christian symbols drawn in the Celtic artistic style. This illustration (left) shows Jesus being arrested. It comes from the Book of Kells.

The Christian religion was introduced to Ireland by St. Patrick in about 450. It spread quickly and it is thanks to the Irish monks, who wrote down many of the myths previously handed on by word of mouth, that we now have so much information about Celtic mythology.

The Celtic cross is a mixture of the Christian cross and a pagan sun disc. The decoration belongs to La Tène tradition.

Due to their superior military organization and strength, the Romans defeated the Celts. But not all the Celtic inhabitants died or fled during the wars of conquest, and as life settled down to peace again, there was a fusion of Roman and Celtic traditions in many areas of daily life. The relief (right), made in Bath after the Roman invasion of Britain, shows a face with typically Celtic features, but surrounded by a Roman-style mane of gorgon hair.

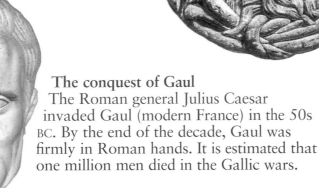

The conquest of Gaul
The Roman general Julius Caesar invaded Gaul (modern France) in the 50s BC. By the end of the decade, Gaul was firmly in Roman hands. It is estimated that one million men died in the Gallic wars.

After defeating the Gauls and invading Britain, Caesar turned homeward to Rome in an attempt to become the supreme Roman ruler. He was declared dictator for life in 44 BC but was murdered shortly afterward.

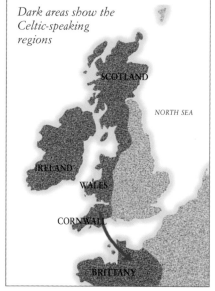

Dark areas show the Celtic-speaking regions

The Celts Live On

From the 5th to 11th centuries the British Isles were invaded first by Anglo-Saxons, then by Vikings and finally by the Normans. Celtic Britons only survived in the most northern and western parts – in Cornwall, Wales, Ireland and the Scottish Highlands. In the following centuries, they too were menaced by the kings of England. However, Celtic traditions survived, and there has even been a revival of Celtic culture and language.

This boy in modern Wales is learning the language of his Celtic forefathers .

Celtic languages lived on in many areas of the British Isles in the centuries after the Roman withdrawal. During the 5th century BC British mercenaries invaded the northern province of Gaul (Brittany), bringing with them a British Celtic dialect spoken at that time in Cornwall. They soon conquered all the lands north of the River Loire and established kingdoms. The area became know as Breton. A modern version of the language they spoke survives in the area to the present day.

King Arthur

Legends about King Arthur came originally from Celtic sources and were very popular during the Middle Ages. In the 12th century a Welsh priest, Geoffrey of Monmouth, wrote down some of the stories and a French poet, Chrétien de Troyes, made them into poems. A German romance of 1212 by Wolfram von Eschenbach tells the tale of the search for the Holy Grail, the cup supposedly used by Christ at the Last Supper.

The tales about King Arthur date from the time of the Anglo-Saxon invasion of Britain, in the 5th to 7th centuries. Historians don't know whether Arthur really existed. In this illustration King Arthur sits with his Knights of the Round Table. Lancelot is on the king's right and Percival on his left. The Round Table stood in the great hall of a legendary castle. Since the table had no head, all the knights seated around it were of equal rank. They were all bound by oath to help each other in times of danger and never to fight among themselves.

Entire families of poverty stricken Celts journeyed across the globe, often taking with them little more than the clothes they stood up in.

Our preservation of some Celtic feast days are just one of the many links with this ancient people. The Celtic festival of Samhain has become All Saint's Day for Roman Catholics, while children in America celebrate the eve as Halloween.

Druids today

In the past decades there has been a worldwide increase of interest in pagan religions and spiritual beliefs of every kind. Interest in the ancient Druids has also revived and there are many groups in Britain today claiming to represent modern Druids. Their interest tends to focus on prehistoric sacred sites, such as Stonehenge and Avebury (although neither has anything at all to do with ancient Druidism), where they hold religious ceremonies.

Celtic migration

During the 18th to 20th centuries, the Celtic areas of the British Isles were shaken again by large-scale migration to the New World. Lairds and English landlords evicted the native population of the Scottish Highlands, who were forced to choose between the slums of large industrial cities in the south or migration to America, Australia or New Zealand. In Ireland, vast population growth combined with the potato blight of 1845–7, encouraged millions of Irish to emigrate. By 1940 over five million Irish had emigrated to the USA alone.

A modern Druid seeking entrance to Stonehenge at Midsummer to perform sacred rights.

This huge white horse is cut into the chalk downs at Uffington in England. Archaeologists are uncertain whether it dates to Celtic times, or whether it was made during the Middle Ages. In either case it remains a mystery, since it is only completely visible from the air.

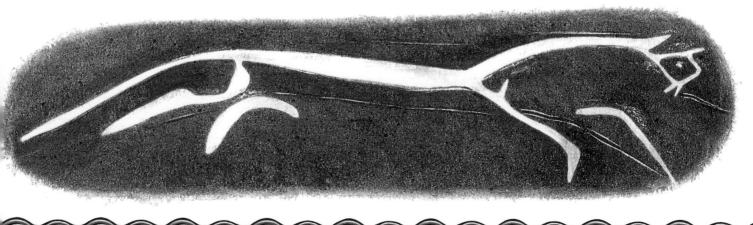

INDEX